ALL THE BEST MEXICAN MEALS

Cookbooks by Joie Warner
ALL THE BEST PASTA SAUCES
ALL THE BEST SALADS
ALL THE BEST PIZZAS
ALL THE BEST CHICKEN DINNERS
ALL THE BEST MEXICAN MEALS
ALL THE BEST MUFFINS AND QUICK BREADS
ALL THE BEST POTATOES
ALL THE BEST COOKIES
ALL THE BEST PASTA SAUCES II
ALL THE BEST RICE
THE COMPLETE BOOK OF CHICKEN WINGS
THE BRAUN HAND BLENDER COOKBOOK
A TASTE OF CHINATOWN
JOIE WARNER'S SPAGHETTI
JOIE WARNER'S CAESAR SALADS
JOIE WARNER'S APPLE DESERTS

ALL THE BEST

MEXICAN MEALS

BY

JOIE WARNER

A FLAVOR BOOK

Copyright © 1992 by Flavor Publications

All rights reserved. No part of this book may be reproduced, stored in a retrieval system, or transmitted in any form or by any means, electronic, mechanical, photocopying, recording or otherwise without prior written permission of the copyright holder.

Published in Canada by

Stoddart Publishing Co. Limited
34 Lesmill Road
Don Mills, Ontario M3B 2T6

CANADIAN CATALOGING IN PUBLICATION DATA
Warner, Joie.
    All the best mexican meals
Includes index.
ISBN 0-7737-5626-4
1. Cookery, Mexican.   I. Title.
TX716.M4W37   1994   641.5972   C93-095337-1

Printed in the United States of America
10 9 8 7 6 5 4 3 2 1

This book was created and produced by

Flavor Publications, Inc.
208 East 51st Street, Suite 240
New York, New York 10022

CONTENTS

INTRODUCTION

ROM SIMPLE BURRITOS and hot, hot chile rellenos to spicy salsas and refreshing Margaritas, Americans are having a love affair with Mexican, Southwestern, and Tex-Mex cooking. The joys of this unique cuisine are that it's festive, vibrant, and exciting to taste; amazingly simple and inexpensive to prepare; wonderfully exotic, yet most of the ingredients are readily available, and – last but not least – it's exceedingly wholesome. Although truly authentic Mexican food can often be elaborate and complicated – what with roasting fresh chiles or preparing homemade tortillas – most of us can prepare tasty facsimiles by using store-bought fresh or frozen tortillas and canned chiles, if fresh or dried aren't available. And while there is no substitute for tomatillos or the aromatic herb cilantro (though, thankfully, many supermarkets now do carry them), other ingredients such as Mexican chocolate and Mexican vanilla can easily be replaced by American products. Most other ingredients – like fresh tomatoes, avocados, dried beans, cumin, limes, oregano, and sesame seeds – can be found in most local supermarkets. So it's not at all difficult to re-create in our own kitchens many of the enticing dishes we have enjoyed in restaurants or while on vacation.

Mexican food is always an adventure to the eyes as well as the palate, no matter how informal or simple the dish. It's honest food that allows the exciting, fresh flavors, textures, and colors of the ingredients to speak for themselves. With their special wholesomeness and visual appeal, the dishes of Mexico, the Southwest, and Tex-Mex too, make perfect sense for both family meals and entertaining. Served simply or buffet-style, each meal is always a celebration of the senses. And, contrary to what many believe, Mexican food is not all hot and spicy. Many dishes have subtle flavors from the comforting pork, chicken, and hominy stew – posole – to creamy, cooling guacamole.

There is no such thing as generic "Mexican" food – it is largely regional cooking based on what ingredients are available locally. However, I have not attempted to write a truly authentic cookbook, since there are a number of excellent cookbooks available that delve into traditional recipes. What I set out to accomplish is simply to create "accessible" recipes that, for the most part, take literally minutes to prepare and, most important, taste fresh and delicious.

I enjoy dissecting traditional recipes, discarding complex techniques – "cheating", if necessary, by using available ingredients – while all the time doing my best to keep the original integrity of the dish. Like most people, I lead a busy, hectic life. Who, today, has time to prepare overly complex dishes except on rare occasions? The question I'm most often asked when people discover my profession is if my recipes are easy. "Can I pick up the ingredients on my way home from work or cook with ingredients I already have on hand? Can I prepare the recipe – from start to finish – in less than 30 minutes?"

That is why *All the Best Mexican Meals* offers quick and simple updated classics and all-time favorite recipes like Guacamole, Chili con Carne, and Margaritas, along with newer creations such as Mexican Meatloaf, Pecan-Crusted Lamb Chops, and Margarita Pie.

Chapter One includes a lively range of appetizers and snacks – everything from quick-to-assemble Mexican Pizza and chile-stuffed olives to Nachos. The second chapter includes soups from refreshing gazpacho and spicy Tortilla Soup to the homey, satisfying Chicken Soup with Whole Corn. Included in the third chapter are scrumptious tortilla dishes such as Chicken Tacos, Sizzling Beef Fajitas, Shrimp Burritos, and Cheese Enchiladas. Another chapter is dedicated to delicious main dishes – look for Mexican Macaroni, Cornmeal Chili Wings, Pork and Chile Stew. Also included are side dishes from the ubiquitous Refried Beans to Corn with Chiles and, of course, delightful classic and modern desserts such as Mexican Wedding Cookies and Mango Mousse and, the favorite of favorites, cooling drinks to serve along with hot and spicy foods or for cocktails on those sultry summer evenings.

Creating a menu with Mexican food is so easy. I've given some serving suggestions but really it's simply a matter of picking and choosing what appetizer or soup to serve with any of the main dishes and then adding side dishes and desserts – whatever appeals to you. As well, many tortilla and main dishes – and soups too – are meals in themselves. Or simply make a meal out of soup and an appetizer – or just an appetizer or two or more.

Along with the recipes, you'll find a glossary to help you find or purchase the freshest and best ingredients. And although it's nice to cook with authentic equipment such as a wooden Mexican bean masher or molcajete – a Mexican mortar and pestle – the recipes in this book were created with no special equipment except perhaps a blender or food processor.

So, if you've always believed Mexican food to be too time-consuming and intimidating to make at home, you're in for a real surprise. I'm sure that once you've prepared some of these spirited, south-of-the-border dishes you'll be well on your way to adopting this fiesta of wonderful tastes as part of your everyday cooking repertoire.

JOIE WARNER

◆ ◆ ◆

INGREDIENTS

AVOCADOS: Always use the greenish-blackish-bumpy skinned Hass avocados for the recipes in this book. They have superior texture and a wonderful nutty taste. An avocado is ripe when it gives a little when pressed gently. Never buy ones with dark, soft spots. If unripe, leave at room temperature for a few days, then refrigerate. Avoid the large, tasteless, smooth-skinned varieties which are more commonly available. Hass avocados are available in some supermarkets and produce stores.

BLACK OLIVES: Here's the one exception where canned black olives – also labelled ripe olives – are "authentic" and preferred over the more pungent Greek Kalamata or French niçoise olives.

CAPERS: These are the unopened flower buds of a Mediterranean shrub. Many cooks prefer the tiny French capers but I use the large variety: they have a stronger flavor. They are packed in vinegar (not salt), and I never rinse them.

CHEDDAR CHEESE: Use best-quality, extra-sharp Cheddar cheese for the recipes in this book.

CHILES: Chiles are one the most important ingredients in Mexican cooking, and there is a bewildering array of varieties – both fresh and dried – each with its own distinctive flavor. However, I have created these recipes using the more readily available – and more convenient – canned chiles (see Jalapeños).

CHILI POWDER: It contains ground dried chiles, cumin, and other seasonings and is available at supermarkets and bulk food stores, though the quality can vary dramatically. I purchase bulk chili powder rather than in the regular spice bottles: the quality is much superior. Some supermarkets carry chili powder in bulk packages.

Try different brands until you find one you like. Many recipes in this book call for several tablespoons of chili powder; if the quality isn't first-rate, the finished dish will taste quite harsh. Pure powdered red chile powder is more authentic, not readily available, and needs to be used in lesser quantities than these recipes specify.

CILANTRO: Also called coriander and Chinese parsley, this pungently aromatic herb is available in Asian and Latin American food shops, some supermarkets, and produce stores. There is no substitute – it really is essential for the recipes in this book. I love cilantro's aroma and taste, but many do not. My solution, when cooking for those who don't adore it, is to leave it out of the recipe altogether and to serve it on the side for people to add as they wish.

DRIED BEANS: The pinto bean, and red and black beans are featured predominately in Mexican cuisine. They can be found dried in most supermarkets, health food and bulk food stores.

FETA CHEESE: Greek feta cheese is used as a substitute for *queso fresco* in these recipes.

GARLIC: Choose large bulbs that are tightly closed and not sprouting. Squeeze the bulb to make sure it is firm and fresh. Powdered garlic should be avoided in any recipes calling for fresh, though it is perfectly acceptable when used with other dried herbs in seasoning mixes for "dry" marinades.

JALAPEÑOS: For convenience, these recipes call for the readily available canned pickled sliced and whole chiles packed in brine (not pickled). Though, normally available in small cans in the Mexican food section of most supermarkets, I purchase huge restaurant-size jars of jalapeños because I use them a lot. Locate a Mexican food wholesaler (restaurant supplier) if you want to purchase large sizes of ingredients such as chiles, tomatillos, et al. – though there is always a required minimum order.

LARD: For true Mexican flavor, real home-rendered lard – not the bland commercial lard – is used in cooking. I use lard only when making beans and refried beans, preferring to use vegetable oil and sometimes butter in my recipes. By the way, lard has about half the cholesterol of butter. To make your own lard, bake about 2 cups chopped pork fat in a 300°F oven for 1 hour, stirring and turning frequently.

LETTUCE: Use either romaine, leaf lettuce, or iceberg for the recipes in this book.

LIMES AND LEMONS: Mexican limes are called limones, but they are not lemons – they're limes. Limes should always be used, though for the sake of convenience I have suggested lemon juice to toss with avocados to prevent them from darkening. But don't substitute lemon juice for lime juice in other recipes. Avoid bottled lime juice.

MONTEREY JACK CHEESE: Sort of a cross between Cheddar and mozzarella cheese with excellent melting qualities, it's available in most supermarkets and specialty cheese shops.

PARMESAN: In these recipes, Parmesan cheese is used as a substitute for Mexican *queso seco* (dry cheese). Be sure to purchase Parmesan that has the words "Parmigiano Reggiano" or second best, "Grana Padano" stamped on the rind. Always grate it fresh just before using: it begins to lose flavor after grating. It is available in Italian food shops or well-stocked cheese stores.

PLANTAIN: A cousin to the banana, it must be cooked before eating. Plantains are found in Caribbean and Latin American food shops and some supermarkets.

SOUR CREAM: I have used sour cream for convenience, but Mexican *crema* is more of a cross between sour cream and the delicate-tasting French *crème fraîche*. To make your own, simply add a few tablespoons of plain, natural yogurt or buttermilk to 1 cup heavy cream and leave covered at room temperature for 24 hours, then refrigerate. Use crema in place of sour cream if desired.

TOMATILLOS: These look like small green tomatoes that are covered in a papery husk; however they are related to the gooseberry – they're not an unripe tomato. I have used the canned variety in these recipes. If you find fresh ones, by all means use them. One pound fresh tomatillos equals about 2 cups canned. Fresh ones must first be husked, then simmered in water until they change from a bright green to a pale, beige green before using.

TOMATOES: Generally, I use cherry tomatoes in these recipes; during most of the year they are more flavorful than out-of-season tomatoes. Leave tomatoes at room temperature for best flavor and to ripen – don't refrigerate unless they begin to overripen. You may substitute ripe, flavorful tomatoes for cherry tomatoes or vice versa: 1 large tomato equals about 12 medium-large cherry tomatoes or about ½ pound.

TOMATOES, CANNED: The best canned tomatoes come from the San Marzano region in Italy, but they are difficult to find. Buy the best Italian or domestic brands available (experiment until you find a brand you like), since this will make an enormous difference in the taste and quality of your sauces. Gently crush them with your hands as you add them to your sauce or crush them in the pan with a wooden spoon if you don't like getting your hands messy.

TORTILLAS: The bread of Mexico, flour and corn tortillas are available in many supermarkets – flour tortillas are sold fresh in plastic packages and corn tortillas are usually in the frozen food section. Many health food stores carry them as well. Store-bought tortillas vary in quality and thickness. I purchase tortillas by the case (900 tortillas!) from a Mexican food manufacturer/wholesaler (restaurant supplier) because they're very fresh, quite thin, and of superior quality. I store them (and give plenty away to friends!) in large freezer bags in the freezer where they last several months.

◆ ◆ ◆

APPETIZERS

♦ ♦ ♦

P lease don't rely on packaged corn chips – homemade tortilla chips are simply so superior. ◆ You may fry them ahead of time and rewarm chips (not if cooked by alternate method) in a very low oven – that's what they do in restaurants to give them that just-made taste.

TORTILLA CHIPS

1 package corn tortillas,   Vegetable oil
    thawed, if frozen   Salt

USING SCISSORS or very sharp knife, cut tortillas into desired shapes (quarters for chips, ¼-inch strips for soup garnishes).

Heat about 1 inch oil in large high-sided skillet to 375°F. Fry tortillas in small batches – do not overcrowd pan or oil will cool, turning chips oily – for about 1 minute or until sizzling stops and they are crisp and golden. Transfer batches to paper towel-lined plate to drain and immediately sprinkle with salt.

Alternately, lightly brush both sides of tortillas with oil, then sprinkle with salt. Cut into desired shapes, place on large baking sheet in single layer, and bake in 450°F oven for 5 minutes or until golden and crisp.

NACHOS

32 homemade tortilla chips (page 14), unsalted
1 cup canned or homemade refried beans (page 79)
I cup grated Monterey Jack cheese (4 ounces)
1 cup grated extra-sharp Cheddar cheese (4 ounces)

¾ cup coarsely diced ripe cherry tomatoes
¼ cup pickled sliced jalapeños, chopped
Chopped cilantro leaves
Sour cream (optional)
Diced avocado (optional)

ADJUST OVEN RACK to top third position; preheat oven to 475°F.

Arrange tortilla chips on ovenproof serving dish or pizza pan in one layer with each one slightly overlapping the other (little or no space between chips). Dollop about 1 teaspoon refried beans on each chip, then sprinkle cheeses evenly over, and scatter tomatoes and chiles on top.

Bake for 5 minutes or until cheese is melted and bubbly. Remove from oven and sprinkle with cilantro and serve at once with separate bowls of sour cream and avocado, if desired. Makes 32 nachos.

N*achos – basically cheese- and chile-topped corn chips – are omnipresent in Mexican and Southwestern eateries. ◆ They're positively yummy and so easy to prepare plus absolutely everyone adores them. ◆ Provide plenty of napkins and serve with Margaritas, Mexican beer, or a pitcher of Sangria (see Index).*

Quesadillas are flour tortillas folded over a filling of grated cheese spiked with chiles or other savory ingredients such as chorizo, vegetables, shredded cooked chicken or meat, then fried or baked. ♦ My favorite filling is simply cheese, chiles, and cilantro, though other times I add diced tomatoes, green onion, and sliced black olives. These savory turnovers make perfect appetizers, hors d'oeuvres, snacks, or a simple lunch.

QUESADILLAS

4 8-inch flour tortillas
1 cup grated Monterey Jack
　cheese (4 ounces)
1 cup grated extra-sharp
　Cheddar cheese
　(4 ounces)

¼ cup pickled sliced
　jalapeños, coarsely
　chopped
¼ cup chopped cilantro
　leaves

HEAT MEDIUM UNGREASED nonstick or heavy skillet over medium-high heat. Add 1 tortilla and sprinkle about ¼ cup of each cheese onto one half, then sprinkle with about 1 tablespoon chiles and a little cilantro. Fold over other half to form half moon. Fry for 1 minute each side or until tortilla is crisp and slightly charred and cheese is melted and beginning to ooze out. (Adjust heat if necessary, but it is important to keep heat fairly high to cook turnovers quickly, otherwise cheese becomes oily and kind of sweet tasting.) Continue until all are completed; keep warm. Cut into wedges and transfer to warmed plates. Serve at once. Makes 4 turnovers.

MEXICAN PIZZA

2 10-inch flour tortillas
1 cup grated Monterey Jack cheese (4 ounces)
1 cup grated extra-sharp Cheddar cheese (4 ounces)
½ pound (about 12 medium) ripe cherry tomatoes, coarsely chopped

¼ cup pickled sliced jalapeños, coarsely chopped
1 large whole green onion, chopped
¼ cup sliced pitted black olives
½ teaspoon dried oregano
¼ cup chopped cilantro leaves

ADJUST OVEN RACK to top third position; preheat oven to 450°F.

Place tortillas side by side on baking sheet large enough to hold them both without touching, or on two 10-inch pizza pans. Sprinkle with equal amounts of each cheese, leaving ½-inch border, then with equal amounts of tomatoes, chiles, green onions, olives, and oregano. Bake for 7 minutes or until cheese is melted and bubbling. Remove from oven and sprinkle with cilantro. Cut into wedges and serve immediately. Serves 2.

Quickly assembled – there's no need to make pizza dough – Mexican pizza is really an open-face quesadilla. ♦ This is just as delicious as the thin-crusted "gourmet" pizzas that are now so in vogue.

P*iquant, marinated seafood makes an absolutely gorgeous opening to a meal or a main-course salad for a summer lunch or dinner.*

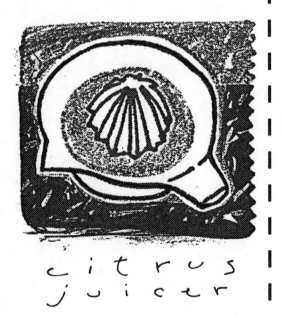

citrus juicer

LIME MARINATED SEAFOOD

1 pound shrimp, peeled and deveined
¼ pound bay scallops
Grated zest of 1 medium lime
¼ cup fresh lime juice
¼ cup olive oil
1 tablespoon Dijon mustard
¼ cup pickled sliced jalapeños, chopped
¼ cup chopped red onion
3 tablespoons diced sweet red pepper
2 tablespoons capers, drained
¼ teaspoon dried oregano
½ teaspoon salt
¼ cup cilantro leaves, chopped, plus extra for garnish
Shredded lettuce

COOK SHRIMP and scallops in boiling water for 1 minute or just until opaque; drain. Combine lime zest, lime juice, oil, mustard, chiles, onion, red pepper, capers, oregano, and salt in medium bowl; stir in shrimp and scallops. Set aside for 15 minutes, stirring occasionally, to allow seafood to absorb flavors, and serve at room temperature; or serve slightly chilled. Stir in cilantro just before serving and spoon onto shredded-lettuce-lined salad plates. Serves 4.

GARLIC CILANTRO SHRIMP

2 large garlic cloves
1 small onion, quartered
¼ cup cilantro leaves
2 tablespoons fresh lime
   juice
½ teaspoon salt
¼ teaspoon cayenne

½ cup (4 ounces/1 stick)
   butter, at room
   temperature
1 pound shrimp, peeled
   and deveined
Lime wedges

PREHEAT OVEN to 400°F.

Chop garlic and onion in food processor. Add cilantro, lime juice, salt, cayenne, and butter and process until well combined.

Arrange shrimp in nonreactive baking dish just large enough to hold them in 1 layer. Spoon mixture over shrimp, toss to coat, and bake for 15 minutes, stirring occasionally, or until opaque; do not overcook. Serve immediately accompanied by lime wedges. Serves 4.

*H*ere, shrimp emerge tasting wonderfully tangy and garlicky. ◆ It might seem like a lot of butter, but when served to several people as an appetizer, accompanied by crusty French bread, there'll be just the right amount for dunking – you'll see! If you don't care to dunk, just throw in another ½ pound of shrimp. ◆ The shrimp are also scrumptious served over White Rice (page 74).

An interesting treatment for canned black olives – stuffing them with chiles, then heightening their flavor by marinating them for a few days.

BLACK OLIVES
STUFFED WITH CHILES

¼ cup olive oil
2 tablespoons red wine
   vinegar
1 garlic clove, very finely
   chopped
½ teaspoon dried oregano
½ teaspoon dried thyme

⅛ teaspoon cayenne
14-ounce can pitted jumbo
   or colossal black olives,
   drained
About 18 small pickled
   jalapeño slices

COMBINE OIL, vinegar, garlic, oregano, thyme, and cayenne in small bowl. Stuff olives with chiles, add to oil mixture, and stir to coat. Cover and refrigerate for 3 days, stirring occasionally. Makes about 18 stuffed olives.

A

ddictive nibbles to serve with ice-cold beer or Margaritas.

HOT AND SPICY PEANUTS

1 tablespoon vegetable oil
2 large garlic cloves, very
  finely chopped
2 cups salted, skinless
  peanuts

1 tablespoon ground cumin
1½ teaspoons cayenne
1 teaspoon salt
1 teaspoon sugar (optional)

HEAT OIL in medium nonstick skillet over medium-high heat. Add garlic and cook for a few seconds. Add peanuts, cumin, cayenne, and salt and stir until thoroughly combined and cook for 1 minute or until fragrant. Remove from heat and stir in sugar if desired. Serve warm or allow to cool and store in an airtight container for up to 2 weeks. Makes 2 cups.

This is Texas-he-man "caviar" served with tortilla chips for scooping. ♦ Make it ahead of time to allow the flavors to blend.

BLACK BEAN CAVIAR

1 cup dried black beans
½ cup finely chopped red onion
2 large garlic cloves, finely chopped
14-ounce can pitted black olives, drained and coarsely chopped
¼ cup olive oil
¼ cup red wine vinegar

½ teaspoon salt
½ teaspoon ground cumin
¼ teaspoon cayenne
¼ cup finely crumbled feta cheese
¼ cup cilantro leaves, chopped
Homemade tortilla chips (page 14)

PLACE BEANS in medium bowl, add water to cover by about 2 inches, and soak overnight; drain beans, discarding soaking water.

Put beans in heavy medium saucepan, add water to cover, and bring to a boil over high heat. Reduce heat, cover, and simmer for 2 hours or until tender; drain and place beans in large bowl. Add onion, garlic, olives, oil, vinegar, salt, cumin, and cayenne and stir until thoroughly combined. Cover and chill. Spoon bean mixture evenly on serving plate. Sprinkle with cheese and cilantro and serve accompanied by tortilla chips. Serves 6 to 8.

CITRUS MARINATED MUSHROOMS

1 pound fresh medium
   mushrooms, stems
   removed
1 cup olive oil
Grated zest of 1 medium
   orange
Grated zest of 1 medium
   lemon
½ cup fresh orange juice
½ cup fresh lemon juice

2 large garlic cloves, very
   finely chopped
2 teaspoons salt
2 teaspoons mustard seed
2 teaspoons dried oregano
2 tablespoons finely
   chopped cilantro leaves
½ teaspoon cayenne
½ teaspoon freshly ground
   black pepper

PLACE MUSHROOMS, oil, orange and lemon zest, and orange and lemon juice in nonreactive saucepan over high heat; bring just to a boil and remove from heat. Transfer mixture to glass jar or bowl, and stir in garlic, salt, mustard seed, oregano, cilantro, cayenne, and pepper. Allow to cool completely, then cover and refrigerate, stirring occasionally, for at least 24 hours before serving. Drain mushrooms and serve. Serves 4.

Mushrooms steeped in a citrus-herb marinade are especially delectable. ◆ Stored in a covered jar and refrigerated, they will keep for up to two weeks – though I'm pretty positive they'll be gobbled up way before then!

Green tomatillos, chiles, and cilantro combine to make a lively, tart-tasting sauce. ◆ Green salsa goes wonderfully well with enchiladas, tostadas, burritos and the like, and is used as a dip for tortilla chips – usually served along with Tomato Salsa (page 25) and Guacamole (page 27).

GREEN CHILE SALSA

2 large garlic cloves
1 medium onion, quartered
2 cups drained canned
  tomatillos

½ cup sliced jalapeños
  (not pickled)
½ cup cilantro leaves
1 teaspoon sugar

CHOP GARLIC and onion in food processor. Add tomatillos, chiles, cilantro, and sugar and process until smooth. Serve at once or chill. Makes about 2 cups.

TOMATO SALSA

1 large garlic clove
1 small onion, quartered
1½ pounds (about 3 large)
   ripe tomatoes, quartered,
   or cherry tomatoes

¼ cup pickled sliced
   jalapeños
½ teaspoon salt
¼ cup chopped cilantro
   leaves

IN FOOD PROCESSOR, coarsely chop garlic and onion. Add tomatoes and chiles and coarsely chop – do not purée. (If using cherry tomatoes there might be a lot of liquid. If so, transfer mixture to strainer and allow most – but not all – of the liquid to drain off, discarding liquid.) Transfer to medium bowl and stir in salt and cilantro. Serve at once. Makes about 2½ cups.

I make my tomato salsa in a food processor being extra careful not to overchop the ingredients. ◆ Salsa fresca must be prepared fresh and served promptly – it doesn't keep well. ◆ This wonderfully fresh-tasting sauce accompanies myriad dishes and is served as a dip with tortilla chips. ◆ If there's someone in your crowd who doesn't adore cilantro, then divide the sauce in half, put it in two separate bowls, and only add cilantro to one.

Blue cheese added to guaca-mole sounds outrageous but it's quite a delightful treat. ◆ Serve with homemade Tortilla Chips (page 14).

BLUE CHEESE GUACAMOLE

2 ripe avocados, halved
   lengthwise and pitted
¼ cup (2 ounces) crumbled
   blue cheese
2 tablespoons fresh lime
   juice

2 tablespoons sour cream
1 teaspoon Worcestershire
   sauce
¼ teaspoon Tabasco
½ teaspoon salt

SCOOP OUT flesh of avocado and place in medium bowl. Gently and coarsely mash avocados with a fork, leaving the mixture somewhat chunky – do not mash perfectly smooth. Add blue cheese, lime juice, sour cream, Worces-tershire sauce, Tabasco, and salt and stir just until com-bined. Serve at once. Makes about 2 cups.

GUACAMOLE

2 ripe avocados, halved lengthwise and pitted
1 tablespoon fresh lemon juice
2 tablespoons chopped pickled jalapeños
1 large garlic clove, finely chopped
1 large whole green onion, chopped
1 ripe medium tomato or 6 cherry tomatoes, coarsely chopped
About ½ teaspoon salt
⅛ teaspoon ground cumin (optional)
¼ cup chopped cilantro leaves

SCOOP OUT FLESH of avocado and place in medium bowl. Gently and coarsely mash avocados with a fork, leaving the mixture somewhat chunky – do not mash perfectly smooth. Add lemon juice, then stir in chiles, garlic, green onion, tomato, salt, cumin, and cilantro. Taste and adjust seasoning and serve at once. Makes about 2½ cups.

Guacamole – an unctuous avocado relish – is served both as a dip with tortilla chips, or as a sauce for tortilla dishes, grilled meats, stews, and soups. ♦ Use only perfectly ripe, Hass avocados – the small, blackish-bumpy-skinned variety – for guacamole. ♦ It is best served immediately, but if you must keep guacamole awhile, cover with plastic wrap, pressing it down to completely cover the surface to prevent darkening, and refrigerate. You may need to scrape off a thin dark layer, or simply stir it into the mixture before serving. ♦ This recipe is easily doubled, but don't double the amount of salt – taste first and only add the desired quantity.

*O*ther soft melting cheeses, such as a combination of grated Monterey Jack, mozzarella, and Muenster cheese, are often used for this simple, tasty appetizer but goat cheese is the most refined.

MELTED CHEESE AND SALSA

12 ounces soft goat cheese (rindless)
Tomato Salsa (page 25)

Homemade tortilla chips (page 14)

PREHEAT OVEN to 450°
Slice goat cheese into 2-inch thick rounds and place in center of 4 heatproof gratin dishes. Bake for 5 minutes or until cheese is hot and bubbling. Place hot dishes on liner plates and allow to stand for 1 minute to cool a little. Spoon salsa around cheese and serve at once with tortilla chips. Serves 4.

Warm Bean Dip

2 tablespoons vegetable oil
¼ cup finely chopped red
   onion
¼ cup pickled sliced
   jalapeños, chopped
2 large garlic cloves, finely
   chopped
1 large ripe tomato or
   8 cherry tomatoes, finely
   chopped
1 tablespoon finely
   chopped cilantro leaves

2 tablespoons fresh lemon
   juice
2 cups canned or
   homemade refried beans
   (page 79)
½ teaspoon best-quality
   chili powder
Homemade tortilla chips
   (page 14)

HEAT OIL in medium saucepan over medium-high heat. Add onion, chiles, garlic, tomato, cilantro, and lemon juice; cook, stirring, for 3 minutes. Add refried beans and chili powder and stir until combined. Reduce heat to medium, cook, stirring, for 4 minutes. Serve warm with tortilla chips. Makes about 2¼ cups.

R*efried beans combined with onion, garlic, tomato, cilantro, and lemon juice make an excellent dip for tortilla chips.*
♦ *Try the dip wrapped inside a warmed flour tortilla, with grated cheese, Tomato Salsa (page 25), and chopped chiles. Or serve as an accompaniment in place of refried beans.*

There are many variations of this hot and spicy pork sausage. Chorizo is a savory filling for tacos, burritos, quesadillas, enchiladas, or delicious served (either crumbled or in patties) alongside scrambled eggs that have been sprinkled with chopped cilantro.

CHORIZO

4 garlic cloves, finely chopped
1 tablespoon red wine vinegar
1 teaspoon sugar
1 teaspoon cayenne
1 teaspoon dried oregano
1 teaspoon salt
½ teaspoon freshly ground black pepper
¼ teaspoon ground cinnamon
¼ teaspoon ground cloves
¼ teaspoon ground cumin
1 pound ground pork

COMBINE GARLIC, vinegar, sugar, cayenne, oregano, salt, pepper, cinnamon, cloves, and cumin in medium bowl. Add ground pork and mix until seasonings are thoroughly incorporated.

If cooking chorizo as a filling, heat ungreased medium nonstick skillet over medium-high heat and cook pork mixture, breaking up meat with a fork, until no pink remains. Tilt pan, remove and discard excess fat, and use sausage as desired.

Or shape chorizo into patties and cook, turning occasionally, until cooked through and lightly browned. Makes 1 pound chorizo or 4 patties.

SOUPS

♦ ♦ ♦

*W*hole corn, summer squash, carrots, and chicken in an herb-flavored stock makes a colorful, nourishing soup. ♦ Add an appetizer, like Quesadillas (page 16), and you have a complete meal.

CHICKEN SOUP WITH WHOLE CORN

8 chicken thighs
2 quarts chicken stock
4 large garlic cloves, finely chopped
1 large onion, chopped
1 tablespoon dried oregano
1 teaspoon best-quality chili powder
6 medium carrots, sliced in half lengthwise, then cut crosswise into 2-inch pieces

3 medium yellow squash or zucchini, cut into ¼-inch slices
3 ears fresh corn, husked and cut into 3 pieces each
1 teaspoon salt
¼ cup cilantro leaves, finely chopped

BRING CHICKEN, chicken stock, garlic, onion, oregano, and chili powder to a boil in large soup pot. Reduce heat, cover, and simmer for 45 minutes or until chicken is tender. Remove chicken with slotted spoon to a plate until cool enough to handle. Skim off most, but not all, surface fat from stock. Tear chicken into large bite-size pieces, discarding skin and bones, and return to pot. Add carrots and bring to a boil. Reduce heat and simmer for 15 minutes or until carrots are tender. Add squash, corn, and salt and cook for 10 minutes or until corn is tender. Sprinkle with cilantro and serve. Serves 6 to 8.

TORTILLA SOUP

6 corn tortillas, cut into
  ¼-inch strips
¼ cup pickled sliced
  jalapeños
½ pound (about
  12 medium) ripe
  cherry tomatoes
1 small onion, quartered
4 large garlic cloves

1 tablespoon vegetable oil
3 cups chicken stock
Grated Monterey Jack
  cheese
Sour cream
Diced avocado tossed with
  a little lemon juice
Chopped cilantro leaves

PREPARE TORTILLA STRIPS (see page 14) but do not salt them.

Purée chiles, tomatoes, onion, and garlic in food processor.

Heat oil in heavy medium saucepan over medium-high heat. Add chile mixture and cook for 4 minutes. Add chicken stock and simmer another 5 minutes. Ladle into warmed wide shallow bowls. Garnish each with a handful of tortilla strips, a sprinkling of cheese, a dollop of sour cream, a little diced avocado, and cilantro leaves. Serve soup with remaining tortilla strips and toppings in separate bowls. Serves 4.

The distinctive earthy taste of crisp tortilla strips added to a chile- and tomato-spiked broth, along with garnishes of cheese, sour cream, avocado, and cilantro, combine to make a delightful bowl of soup bursting with Mexican flavors.

T hick and hearty, this soup is a meal in itself. ♦ The perfect accompaniment is home-made tortilla chips (page 14) or corn muffins (see recipe in my book, All the Best Muffins and Quick Breads). ♦ Some recipes include ground cumin – you may add it to taste if you like.

BLACK BEAN SOUP

2 cups (1 pound) dried black beans, rinsed and debris removed
2 tablespoons olive or vegetable oil
1 large onion, chopped
6 large garlic cloves, chopped
1 tablespoon chopped pickled jalapeños
8 cups chicken stock
1 tablespoon dried oregano
1 teaspoon dried thyme
1 bay leaf
¼ teaspoon ground cloves
2 tablespoons chopped pickled jalapeños
Salt
Sour cream
Ripe cherry tomatoes, coarsely chopped
Chopped cilantro leaves or green onions
Lime wedges

PLACE BEANS in large bowl, add water to cover by about 2 inches, and soak overnight; drain beans, discarding soaking water.

Heat oil in large heavy saucepan over medium-high heat. Add onion, garlic, chiles, and cook for 2 minutes or until tender. Add drained beans and chicken stock, reduce heat, and simmer for 1 hour. Add oregano, thyme, bay leaf, cloves, and chiles and continue to simmer for another 30 minutes or until tender. Remove bay leaf.

Purée 2 cups of cooked beans in food processor, then return to soup. Add salt to taste. Ladle into warmed wide shallow bowls, garnish with sour cream, tomatoes, and cilantro and serve with lime wedges. Serves 8.

FRESH TOMATO GAZPACHO

1 large garlic clove
1 small red onion, quartered
4 ripe medium tomatoes (1 pound), seeded and quartered
1¼ cups (10-ounce can) tomato juice
1 tablespoon red wine vinegar
½ teaspoon sugar
½ teaspoon salt
½ teaspoon dried oregano
⅛ teaspoon cayenne
Diced peeled cucumber
Diced sweet red pepper
Sliced pitted black olives
Diced avocado tossed with a little lemon juice
Chopped cilantro leaves
Chopped fresh mint leaves

COARSELY CHOP GARLIC and onion in food processor. Add tomatoes, tomato juice, vinegar, sugar, salt, oregano, and cayenne and purée until smooth. Put in nonreactive bowl; chill several hours before serving.

Put remaining ingredients in separate bowls and pass toppings to be added according to individual taste. Serves 4.

ummertime is the best time to make and serve this refreshing soup. Ripe, flavorful tomatoes are absolutely essential. ♦ *The soup must chill for several hours, so plan accordingly.*

chile

TORTILLA DISHES

◆ ◆ ◆

Chilaquiles – the name for this dish – means "the ragged straws of a broken sombrero." ♦ Traditionally, this humble – and surprisingly scrumptious – dish was a way to use up stale tortillas. ♦ Enjoy as a simple lunch, or serve it for a late breakfast or brunch with a poached egg on top, with refried beans, and perhaps glasses of Sangria (page 90).

TORTILLA HASH WITH CHORIZO

8 corn tortillas, cut into ¼-inch strips
Chorizo (page 30)
2 large (1 pound) ripe tomatoes, quartered, or cherry tomatoes
¼ cup sliced pickled jalapeños

¼ cup chicken stock
¼ cup freshly grated Parmesan cheese plus extra for garnish
Sour cream
Chopped cilantro leaves
Chopped green onion

PREPARE TORTILLA STRIPS (see page 14) but do not salt them.

Prepare chorizo; purée tomatoes and chiles in food processor and add to chorizo along with chicken stock, cheese, and tortilla strips. Bring to a boil over medium-high heat, stirring mixture very gently to combine. Cook for 2 minutes or until tortilla strips have softened and most of the liquid is absorbed; do not overcook – mixture still should be moist and tortillas not mushy. Serve chilaquiles in warmed wide shallow bowls, garnish with sour cream, cilantro, green onion, and Parmesan cheese. Serves 4 to 6.

CHICKEN TACOS

Vegetable oil
2 large garlic cloves,
   chopped
3 skinless, boneless
   chicken breast halves, cut
   into 2 x ¼-inch strips
1 teaspoon dried oregano
¾ teaspoon ground cumin
Salt

8 corn tortillas
Tomato Salsa (page 25)
Shredded lettuce
Chopped green onion
Chopped cilantro leaves
Diced avocado tossed with
   a little lemon juice
Several sliced pitted black
   olives

HEAT 1 TABLESPOON oil in large nonstick skillet over medium-high heat. Add garlic and cook for a few seconds. Add chicken, oregano, cumin, and salt and cook for 3 minutes or until cooked through; keep warm.

Lightly brush 1 side of tortillas with oil. Heat medium nonstick skillet over medium-high heat and cook tortillas, one at a time, for a few seconds each side or just until softened – not crisp.

Place warm tortillas and chicken filling on separate warmed serving dishes. Put remaining ingredients in separate bowls. To eat, each person takes a tortilla, spoons a little of the chicken filling down the center, garnishes with toppings, then folds it in half and eats it like a sandwich. Makes 8 tacos.

D*elicious tacos wrapped around shredded chicken, then splashed with piquant salsa and garnished with lettuce, green onions, cilantro, avocado, and olives, taste as fresh as a salad. ◆ Provide plenty of napkins.*

T he addition of cream makes these chicken– and cheese-stuffed enchiladas utterly rich and delicious. ◆ The bowls of colorful fresh vegetable toppings and cooling sour cream add pleasing contrasts.

CREAMY CHICKEN ENCHILADAS

3 chicken breast halves
1 large garlic clove
½ cup pickled sliced jalapeños
½ pound (about 12 medium) ripe cherry tomatoes
¾ cup heavy cream
¼ cup freshly grated Parmesan cheese
Vegetable oil
8 corn tortillas
½ cup grated Monterey Jack cheese (2 ounces)

1 large green onion, chopped
¼ cup chopped cilantro leaves
1 cup grated combination of Monterey Jack and Cheddar cheese (4 ounces)
Shredded lettuce
Guacamole (page 27)
Sour cream
Chopped cherry tomatoes
Several sliced black olives
Cilantro leaves

PREHEAT OVEN to 400°F.

Place chicken in baking dish and bake for 20 minutes or until cooked through. When cool enough to handle, tear chicken into shreds, discarding skin and bones.

Purée garlic, chiles, tomatoes, cream, and Parmesan cheese in food processor.

Lightly brush 1 side of tortillas with oil. Heat medium nonstick skillet over medium-high heat and cook tortillas, one at a time, for a few seconds or just until softened – not crisp.

Reduce oven heat to 375°F.

Divide chicken shreds, Monterey Jack cheese, green onion, and cilantro evenly onto each tortilla, then spoon about 1 tablespoon sauce mixture over each one. Roll up tortillas and place seam side down in 7 × 11-inch glass baking dish. Pour remaining sauce over enchiladas, sprinkle with combined cheese and bake for 30 minutes or until heated through. Serve enchiladas topped with a little shredded lettuce, a dollop of guacamole and sour cream, cherry tomatoes, olives, and cilantro. Serve additional toppings in separate bowls. Serves 4.

green onion

C heese enchiladas are very simple to prepare and very tasty. If you prefer a darker-colored sauce, add chili powder to taste when adding the oregano and cumin to the sauce. Serve with Refried Beans (page 79) and/or Mexican Red Rice (page 72).

CHEESE ENCHILADAS

Vegetable oil
4 corn tortillas
1 cup grated extra-sharp
  Cheddar cheese
  (4 ounces)
1 cup grated Monterey Jack
  cheese (4 ounces)
1 large green onion,
  chopped
¼ cup chopped cilantro
  leaves
1 large garlic clove, finely
  chopped

1 tablespoon chopped
  pickled jalapeños
2 tablespoons all-purpose
  flour
¾ cup chicken stock
1 teaspoon dried oregano
⅛ teaspoon ground cumin
A few sliced pitted black
  olives
Sour cream
Guacamole (page 27), or
  diced avocado tossed
  with a little lemon juice

PREHEAT OVEN to 375°F.

Lightly brush one side of tortillas with oil. Heat medium nonstick skillet over medium-high heat and cook tortillas, one at a time, for a few seconds each side or until softened – not crisp.

Combine two cheeses, reserving ½ cup for topping. Place equal amount of cheese mixture just off center on each tortilla and sprinkle equally with green onion and cilantro. Roll fairly tightly and place 1 to 2 tortillas – seam side down – on each heatproof plate, or use gratin dishes or a nonstick baking dish.

Heat 2 tablespoons oil in medium nonstick skillet over medium-high heat. Add garlic and chiles and cook for 1 minute. Stir in flour and cook, stirring constantly, for 4 minutes or until golden colored. Whisk in chicken stock, oregano, and cumin and bring to a boil, whisking constantly. Simmer until thickened, then spoon equal amounts of sauce over enchiladas and sprinkle with remaining cheese. Top with olives and bake for 10 minutes or until cheese is melted and sauce bubbling; do not overcook. Place hot dishes on liner plates and serve with sour cream and guacamole. Serves 2 to 4.

leaf
lettuce

A *savory filling for tacos, tostadas, chimichangas, and enchiladas.*

BEEF CHILE SAUCE

1 tablespoon vegetable oil
1½ pounds ground beef
2 medium onions, chopped
4 large garlic cloves, chopped
14-ounce can Italian plum tomatoes, undrained
¼ cup pickled sliced jalapeños, coarsely chopped

2 tablespoons best-quality chili powder
1 tablespoon dried oregano
½ teaspoon salt
⅛ teaspoon ground cloves

HEAT OIL in large nonstick skillet over medium-high heat. Add beef and cook, breaking up meat with fork, until no pink remains. Tilt pan and spoon out excess oil; transfer ground beef to a plate.

Add onions and garlic to skillet and cook for 2 minutes or until tender. Return beef and add remaining ingredients. Cook, stirring frequently, for 20 minutes or until liquid is absorbed but mixture is still moist. Makes enough filling for about 14 tacos.

BEEF TACOS

Beef Chile Sauce (page 44)
14 corn tortillas
Vegetable oil
Grated extra-sharp
  Cheddar cheese

Shredded lettuce
Tomato Salsa (page 25)
Sour cream
Chopped cilantro leaves

PREPARE BEEF CHILE SAUCE; keep warm.

Lightly brush one side of tortillas with oil. Heat medium nonstick skillet over medium-high heat and cook tortillas, one at a time, for a few seconds each side or just until softened – not crisp.

Place warm tortillas and beef chile sauce on separate warmed serving dishes. Put remaining ingredients in separate bowls. To eat, each person takes a tortilla, then spoons a little of the beef filling down the center, garnishes with toppings, then folds it in half and eats it like a sandwich. Makes 14 tacos.

acos are probably the most familiar Mexican dish throughout America and a ground-beef filling the most popular. ◆ In Mexico, fillings reflect the regional cuisine – from wonderful seafood to charcoal-grilled meats and poultry – never ground beef. A Southwestern creation I'm sure, a ground-beef filling is, nonetheless, irresistibly delicious.

One of the mistaken notions many people have about Mexican cuisine is that it's all hot and spicy. This incredibly easy-to-make and surprisingly delicious – don't let the simple ingredients fool you – dish is not. ♦ Here, flour tortillas are wrapped around a filling of refried beans, then sprinkled with cheese, and quickly baked. What brings this humble dish to life is the colorful toppings: sour cream, salsa, and chopped cilantro and green onions.

BEAN BURRITOS

4 8-inch flour tortillas
2 cups canned or
  homemade refried beans
  (page 79)
1 cup grated extra-sharp
  Cheddar cheese
  (4 ounces)

1 cup grated Monterey Jack
  cheese (4 ounces)
Sour cream
Tomato Salsa (page 25)
Chopped cilantro leaves
Chopped whole green
  onions

SPRINKLE EACH TORTILLA with a little water, wrap them completely in foil, and place in 300°F oven for 15 minutes to soften. Remove from oven; raise heat to 400°F.

Spoon about ½ cup refried beans about ½ inch in on bottom of each softened tortilla. Roll up jelly-roll style until tortilla is log-shaped. Place 1 burrito seam side down on each of 4 heatproof plates (or place all of them in nonstick baking dish). Sprinkle them with equal amounts of cheese. Bake for 8 minutes or until cheese is melted and bean mixture is heated through; be careful not to overcook or tortillas will crisp instead of remaining soft. Place hot dishes on liner plates and serve. Put remaining ingredients in separate bowls and pass toppings for each person to add as they wish. Serves 4.

CHIMICHANGAS

8 10-inch flour tortillas
1 cup canned or
 homemade refried beans
 (page 79)
1 cup grated extra-sharp
 Cheddar cheese
 (4 ounces)
1 cup grated Monterey Jack
 cheese (4 ounces)
½ cup pickled sliced
 jalapeños, chopped

Salt
Dried oregano
Vegetable oil
Shredded lettuce
Sour cream
Guacamole (page 27)
Tomato Salsa (page 25) or
 chopped cherry tomatoes
Chopped cilantro leaves

SPRINKLE EACH TORTILLA with a little water, wrap them completely in foil, and place in 300°F oven for 15 minutes to soften.

Spoon a few tablespoons refried beans in center of each tortilla. Sprinkle with equal amounts of each cheese, then chiles, a little salt and a pinch of oregano. Fold opposite sides of tortilla over mixture, then fold over the top and bottom, and secure with wooden toothpicks.

Heat about 1 inch oil in large nonstick skillet to 360°F. Fry parcels, about 3 at a time, for 1 minute each side or until golden and crisp. Transfer to paper towel-lined plate to drain; keep warm while completing remaining ones. Remove toothpicks.

Arrange shredded lettuce on plates and place 1 to 2 chimichangas on each. Place remaining ingredients in separate bowls and garnish chimichangas with a little of each topping. Pass remaining toppings for each person to add as they wish. Serves 4 to 8.

Tortilla parcels wrapped around a refried beans-and-cheese filling make delightful eats. You may also fill them with Beef Chile Sauce (page 44), Carnitas (page 66), or Picadillo (page 52). As well, you can fry them ahead of time and reheat in a 400°F oven for 8 minutes or until crisp and filling is hot.

Brought to the table sizzling for dramatic effect, beef fajitas are a deservedly popular dish in Mexican restaurants. ♦ Charbroiling is by far the best method of cooking the steaks, but they can be broiled quite successfully.

SIZZLING BEEF FAJITAS

2 large garlic cloves, finely chopped
1 tablespoon vegetable oil
¼ cup fresh lime juice
¼ cup soy sauce
¼ cup Worcestershire sauce
1 pound skirt steak or top sirloin, trimmed, cut in half crosswise
8 8-inch flour tortillas
1 large onion, thinly sliced

1 large sweet green pepper, seeded and cut into ¼-inch strips
1 large sweet red pepper, seeded and cut into ¼-inch strips
Salt
Freshly ground black pepper
Guacamole (page 27)
Tomato Salsa (page 25)
Sour cream

COMBINE GARLIC, oil, lime juice, soy sauce, and Worcestershire sauce in shallow glass or nonreactive dish just large enough to hold meat in 1 layer. Add meat to marinade, turn several times to coat; cover, and refrigerate for 3 hours, turning occasionally.

Prepare charcoal fire.

Sprinkle each tortilla with a little water, wrap them completely in foil, and place in 300°F oven for 15 minutes to soften. When coals are red-hot, remove meat from marinade and place on lightly oiled grill. Grill for 5 minutes each side or until medium-rare. Transfer to cutting surface; keep warm.

While steaks are grilling, heat large cast-iron skillet over medium-high heat. Add onion and peppers and cook, stirring frequently, for 5 minutes or until tender and lightly charred; remove pan from heat but don't turn off heat. Cut meat into thin strips against the grain on the diagonal, sprinkle with salt and pepper, and place on top of vegetables in skillet. Place skillet back on high heat for 1 minute, drizzle over 2 tablespoons marinade, then immediately bring to the table "sizzling" and place on a trivet. Put remaining ingredients in separate bowls and serve with warmed tortillas. Serves 4.

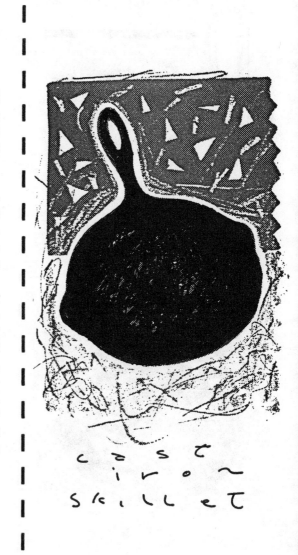

cast iron skillet

P

iled high with shredded lettuce, refried beans, guacamole, crabmeat, cheese, green salsa, tomatoes, and olives, this Mexican-style open-face sandwich is festive and fun. ◆ Try different fillings – cooked chicken, Chorizo (page 30), or Carnitas (page 66) in place of crabmeat – though crabmeat is the ultimate.

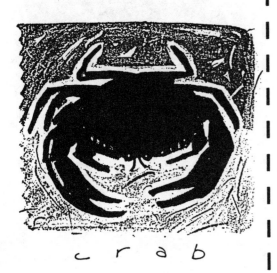

crab

CRAB TOSTADAS

Vegetable oil
6 corn tortillas
2 teaspoons red wine vinegar
2 cups shredded lettuce
1 cup canned or homemade refried beans (page 79)
Guacamole (page 27)
1 pound cooked crabmeat
½ cup Green Chile Salsa (page 24) plus extra for serving

1 cup grated extra-sharp Cheddar cheese (4 ounces)
About 8 ripe cherry tomatoes, coarsely chopped
Several sliced pitted black olives
Cilantro leaves

HEAT ABOUT ¼ INCH OIL in medium nonstick skillet and fry tortillas, one at a time, until crisp and golden; remove to a paper towel-lined plate to drain; keep warm. Alternately, lightly brush both sides of tortillas with oil, place them in 1 layer without overlapping on large baking sheet, and bake in 400°F oven for 5 minutes or until crisp and golden.

Combine 2 tablespoons vegetable oil and vinegar in medium bowl; add lettuce and toss to combine.

Place tortillas on 6 dinner plates. Layer each equally with beans, leaving ¼-inch border, then guacamole, lettuce mixture, crabmeat, green chile salsa, cheese, tomatoes, olives, and top with cilantro. Serve with extra green chile salsa. Serves 6.

SHRIMP BURRITOS

6 8-inch flour tortillas
1 pound medium shrimp
  with shell on
½ pound (about 12
  medium) cherry
  tomatoes, coarsely
  chopped
Diced avocado
2 tablespoons lime juice
1 large garlic clove, finely
  chopped

1 whole green onion,
  chopped
2 tablespoons chopped
  cilantro leaves
2 tablespoons chopped
  pickled jalapeños
Shredded lettuce
Sour cream

SPRINKLE EACH TORTILLA with a little water, wrap them completely in foil, and place in 300°F oven for 15 minutes to soften.

Cook shrimp in salted boiling water for 2 minutes or until opaque; do not overcook. Drain; run under cold running water to stop cooking, and drain again. Peel and devein shrimp.

Toss tomatoes, avocado, lime juice, garlic, green onion, cilantro, and chiles in medium bowl.

Spoon equal amounts shrimp and avocado mixture onto center of each tortilla. Add shredded lettuce and a dollop of sour cream. Fold opposite sides of tortilla over mixture, overlapping, then fold up bottom and place seam side down on plates. Serve at once. Serves 3 to 6.

he combination of shrimp, avocado salad, lettuce, and sour cream produces a fresh-tasting, satisfying dish. ◆ You may cook the shrimp ahead of time, but the avocado salad must be made just prior to serving.

A sweet and spicy ground beef filling for tacos or burritos, or serve with White Rice (page 74). ♦ Serve with toppings of sour cream, salsa, and cheese if desired.

PICADILLO

2 tablespoons vegetable oil
2 large garlic cloves, chopped
1 medium onion, chopped
1 pound ground beef
2 large (1 pound) ripe tomatoes or cherry tomatoes, chopped
2 tablespoons cider vinegar
1 teaspoon sugar
1 teaspoon salt
1 teaspoon ground cinnamon
½ teaspoon ground cumin
½ teaspoon cayenne
⅛ teaspoon ground cloves
½ cup pimiento-stuffed olives, sliced
¼ cup slivered almonds, lightly toasted
¼ cup raisins
¼ cup cilantro leaves, chopped

HEAT OIL in large nonstick skillet over medium-high heat. Add garlic and onion and cook for 2 minutes or until tender. Add beef and cook, breaking up meat with a fork, until no pink remains; drain off fat. Stir in tomatoes, vinegar, sugar, salt, cinnamon, cumin, cayenne, and cloves; cover, reduce heat, and simmer for 10 minutes to absorb flavors. Add olives, almonds, raisins, and cilantro and serve. Serves 4.

RANCH-STYLE EGGS

2 corn tortillas or 8-inch flour tortillas	Chili powder
Butter	Tomato Salsa (page 25)
½ cup canned or homemade refried beans (page 79)	Sour cream
	Freshly grated Parmesan cheese
2 to 4 large eggs	Diced avocado tossed with a little lemon juice
Salt	Chopped cilantro leaves

LIGHTLY BRUSH CORN TORTILLAS with butter. Heat medium nonstick skillet over medium-high heat and cook tortillas, one at a time, for a few seconds each side or just until softened – not crisp; keep warm. If using flour tortillas, sprinkle each tortilla with a little water, wrap them completely in foil, and place in 300°F oven for 15 minutes to soften.

In small saucepan, heat refried beans; keep warm.

Melt 2 tablespoons butter in large nonstick skillet over medium heat. Add eggs and sprinkle with a little salt and chili powder. Fry sunny side up until whites are set and yolks are heated through but still soft.

Place 1 tortilla on each warmed plate, place 1 or 2 eggs in center, and encircle eggs with salsa. Garnish each plate with a dollop of sour cream, a dollop of refried beans sprinkled with Parmesan cheese, and some diced avocado. Sprinkle eggs with cilantro and serve at once. Serves 2.

H*uevos rancheros, a hearty egg dish classic to both Mexican and Southwestern cuisine, is both beautiful to look at and delicious to eat.* ♦ *This makes a memorable breakfast or lunch accompanied by an exquisite Tequila Sunrise (page 91)* ♦ *Most supermarket eggs are flavorless – perfectly fine for baking but totally tasteless. Try to obtain farm-fresh eggs for best flavor.*

cilantro

MAIN DISHES

◆ ◆ ◆

S uffused with orange, this marinated chicken is wonderfully moist and succulent. It can be baked in a 425°F oven with excellent results, too. ◆ Serve, if you like, with Zucchini, Corn, and Red Pepper Sauté (page 81).

GRILLED ORANGE CHICKEN

4 large garlic cloves, chopped
1 small onion, chopped
Grated zest of 1 large orange
1 cup fresh orange juice
2 tablespoons Cointreau
1 tablespoon vegetable oil
1 teaspoon cayenne
½ teaspoon dried thyme
¼ teaspoon salt
6 chicken pieces – thighs, legs, breasts

COMBINE GARLIC, onion, orange zest, orange juice, Cointreau, oil, cayenne, thyme, and salt in nonreactive dish just large enough to hold chicken in 1 layer. Add chicken and turn several times to coat. Cover, and marinate in refrigerator overnight, turning occasionally.

Prepare charcoal fire and when coals are red-hot, remove chicken from marinade and place on lightly oiled grill. Grill, turning and basting frequently with marinade, for 15 minutes or until cooked through. Serves 3 to 6.

TABLECLOTH STAINER CHICKEN

Vegetable oil
3-pound chicken, cut up
  and skin removed
6 large garlic cloves,
  chopped
1 large onion, chopped
2 tablespoons all-purpose
  flour
¼ cup pickled sliced
  jalapeños, chopped
1 teaspoon dried oregano
½ teaspoon cayenne
¼ teaspoon salt

¼ teaspoon ground
  cinnamon
14-ounce can plum
  tomatoes, undrained
2 cups chicken stock
1 large ripe plantain or
  2 firm bananas, peeled
  and sliced
2 tart apples, peeled, cored,
  and diced
1 cup cubed, pared fresh
  pineapple (not canned)
Chopped cilantro leaves

HEAT 2 TABLESPOONS oil in heavy Dutch oven over medium-high heat. Brown chicken in batches and remove to a plate.

Remove all but 2 tablespoons oil, add garlic and onion and cook for 2 minutes. Stir in flour and cook, stirring constantly, for 2 minutes more. Add chiles, oregano, cayenne, salt, cinnamon, tomatoes, including liquid, and chicken stock; bring to a boil. Add chicken, reduce heat, cover, and simmer 45 minutes or until tender. Remove chicken with slotted spoon to plate, turn heat to high, and cook sauce for 4 minutes or until slightly thickened.

In medium nonstick skillet, heat thin film oil and cook plantains (if using bananas omit this step) for 4 minutes or until golden. Add plantain or bananas, apples, pineapple, and chicken to stew to heat through. Transfer to serving dish and sprinkle with cilantro. Serves 4.

Whimsically named, mancha manteles de pollo carries a fair warning: do not use your best table linens! ♦ Serve with White Rice (page 74).

C hicken in mole sauce is one of Mexico's most famous and exotic dishes. ◆ Traditionally made with turkey or cut-up whole chicken, I prefer chicken thighs. ◆ Serve with White Rice (page 74) and Fried Plantains (page 80).

CHICKEN IN CHILE CHOCOLATE SAUCE

2 large garlic cloves
1 small onion, quartered
1 cup chicken stock
1 corn tortilla, cut into small pieces
¼ cup sliced pickled jalapeños
¼ cup sesame seeds, lightly toasted, reserving 2 tablespoons for garnish
¼ cup slivered almonds, lightly toasted
2 tablespoons raisins

1 tablespoon sugar
1 teaspoon dried oregano
¼ teaspoon ground cinnamon
2 tablespoons vegetable oil
8 skinless chicken thighs
19-ounce can Italian plum tomatoes, undrained
½ square (½ ounce) unsweetened chocolate
¼ cup chopped cilantro leaves

CHOP GARLIC and onion in food processor. Add chicken stock, tortilla, chiles, sesame seeds, almonds, raisins, sugar, oregano, and cinnamon; purée mixture.

Heat oil in large nonstick skillet over medium-high heat. Brown chicken in batches; remove to a plate. Add puréed mixture and tomatoes, including liquid, to skillet; reduce heat to low, add chocolate and stir to melt. Add chicken, raise heat to medium-low, cover, and cook for 45 minutes, turning occasionally, or until tender. Stir in cilantro, transfer to warmed platter, and sprinkle with sesame seeds. Serves 4 to 8.

CORNMEAL CHILI WINGS

2½ pounds chicken wings
2 tablespoons yellow
  cornmeal
2 teaspoons best-quality
  chili powder

1 teaspoon garlic powder
1 teaspoon cayenne
1 teaspoon salt

PREHEAT OVEN to 450°F.

Trim wings: cut off wing tips and save for stock or discard. Cut away "triangle" of skin between the two sections, then cut each wing into two parts.

Thoroughly blend cornmeal, chili powder, garlic powder, cayenne, and salt in large bowl. Toss wings in mixture until evenly coated. Arrange wings skin side up in a single layer on lightly greased rack set over baking sheet, or on broiling rack with bottom pan. Bake for 30 minutes, without turning, or until cooked through and skin is crisp. Serves 2.

S picy, Southwestern wings are simply tossed with a dry marinade before baking. ◆ Serve with Corn, Chile, and Tomato Salsa (page 77) or Corn with Chiles (page 76), and a baked sweet potato, if desired.

M y version of this immensely popular hot and spicy stew is traditional – no beans, no tomatoes, cubed beef instead of ground – except that I cheat and use bottled hot sauce! Purists would call this heresy, I know. But I don't care 'cause it sure tastes good! The essence of this stew is the chili powder so, please, use only the best.

CHILI CON CARNE

3 tablespoons vegetable oil
3 pounds boneless top sirloin steak, trimmed and cut into ½-inch cubes
10 large garlic cloves, coarsely chopped
1 medium onion, chopped
2 cups beef stock
1 heaping tablespoon dried oregano
7 tablespoons best-quality chili powder

6 tablespoons Durkee Frank's Red Hot Sauce
3 tablespoons yellow cornmeal
Sour cream
Grated extra-sharp Cheddar cheese
Ripe cherry tomatoes, coarsely chopped
Chopped cilantro leaves
Chopped green onions
Homemade tortilla chips (page 14)

HEAT 2 TABLESPOONS OIL in large nonstick skillet over medium-high heat. Brown beef in several batches – do not overcrowd or beef will steam instead of brown – and remove to a plate.

Add 1 tablespoon oil, garlic, and onion to skillet and cook for 2 minutes or until tender. Add beef stock, oregano, chili powder, hot sauce, and beef and any juices. Reduce heat to medium-low, cover, and simmer for 20 minutes. Remove cover, stir in cornmeal, raise heat to medium and simmer for 10 minutes or until slightly thickened.

Place remaining ingredients in separate bowls. Spoon stew into warmed wide shallow bowls and garnish each serving with a little of the toppings and place a few tortilla chips around edges. Pass remaining toppings for each person to add as they wish. Serves 4.

PECAN-CRUSTED LAMB CHOPS

1 cup chopped pecans	⅛ teaspoon salt
2 large garlic cloves, finely chopped	8 loin lamb chops about 1-inch thick
⅓ cup Dijon mustard	3 tablespoons butter

PLACE PECANS on a plate. Combine garlic, mustard, and salt in small bowl. Spread both sides of lamb chops with mustard mixture, then dip them into chopped nuts to coat both sides. Press to help nuts adhere.

Melt butter in large nonstick skillet over high heat. Add lamb chops, and reduce heat to medium. Cook for about 6 minutes each side – turning carefully with tongs to keep nut coating intact – or until rare or done to taste. Be careful not to burn nut coating or it will be bitter; reduce heat if necessary.

Serve at once on warmed plates. Serves 4.

L amb seasoned with a mustard-pecan topping is an intriguing combination of flavors and textures. ◆ You may prepare the lamb chops several hours ahead, cover, and refrigerate, but bring them back to room temperature before cooking. ◆ A simple side dish is Corn with Chiles (page 76).

Grilling the steak and vegetables is what makes this dish special: I don't recommend broiling in this instance. ◆ Serve the steak and vegetables with separate small side dishes of refried beans that have been sprinkled with a little grated Cheddar and Monterey Jack cheese and heated in the oven or microwave until the cheese is melted.

GRILLED STEAK WITH CHARRED ONIONS AND PEPPERS

2 medium onions, sliced about ⅝-inches thick, keeping rings intact
2 small sweet red peppers, cut in thick rings
Olive or vegetable oil
Salt
2 New York strips, T-bones, or ribeye steaks (at least 1-inch thick)

PREPARE CHARCOAL FIRE and when coals are red-hot brush both sides of onions and peppers with oil and sprinkle with salt. Grill vegetables for 6 minutes or until lightly charred and tender. Remove from grill; keep warm.

Brush steaks with oil and sprinkle with salt and grill steaks for 4 minutes each side or until medium rare or done to taste. Transfer steaks to warmed platter and let rest for 4 minutes. Top steaks with grilled vegetables and serve. Serves 2.

MEXICAN MEATLOAF

1 pound lean ground beef
1 pound ground veal
¾ cup pitted black olives,
    coarsely chopped
½ cup yellow cornmeal
2 large eggs, lightly beaten
1 medium onion, chopped
¼ cup pickled sliced
    jalapeños, chopped

2 large garlic cloves,
    chopped
1 teaspoon best-quality
    chili powder
1 teaspoon dried oregano
1 teaspoon salt

PREHEAT OVEN to 350°F. Combine all ingredients in large bowl (hands work best for mixing). Gently pack mixture into greased 9 x 5 x 3-inch loaf pan. Bake for 1 hour and 15 minutes or just until cooked through. Serves 8.

Seasoned with cornmeal, chiles, and olives, this is a spicy, Southwestern rendition of meatloaf. ◆ Hot pepper jelly makes a delicious accompaniment, or brush on the jelly while it's baking to glaze the meatloaf.

P osole is a delicious, satisfying Mexican stew named after posole or corn that has been removed from the cob and specially treated, then dried. ◆ Many cooks – myself included – substitute the more readily available canned hominy.

PORK, CHICKEN, AND HOMINY STEW

3 pounds boneless pork shoulder or butt, trimmed and cut into ½-inch cubes
6 chicken thighs
2 quarts chicken stock
4 large garlic cloves, chopped
1 large onion, chopped
1 tablespoon dried oregano
1 teaspoon best-quality chili powder
¼ cup pickled sliced jalapeños, chopped

3 cans (14.5-ounces each) hominy, undrained
Tomato Salsa (page 25), or chopped ripe cherry tomatoes
Guacamole (page 27), or diced ripe avocado tossed with a little lime juice
Chopped cilantro leaves
Chopped green onion
Quartered limes

BRING PORK, chicken, chicken stock, garlic, onion, oregano, chili powder, and chiles to a boil in large soup pot. Reduce heat to medium-low, cover, and simmer for 1 hour or until pork is tender. Remove from heat and transfer chicken with slotted spoon to plate until cool enough to handle. Skim off most, but not all, surface fat from stock.

Tear chicken into large bite-size pieces, discarding skin and bones, and return to pot. Add hominy including liquid from two cans, discarding liquid from third can. Reheat thoroughly and serve hot in warmed wide bowls. Put remaining ingredients in separate bowls and pass toppings to be added to individual taste. Serves 8.

PORK AND CHILE STEW

2 tablespoons vegetable oil
3 pounds boneless pork
   shoulder or butt,
   trimmed and cut into
   ½-inch cubes
4 large garlic cloves,
   chopped
1 large onion, thinly sliced
2 tablespoons all-purpose
   flour

2½ cups chicken stock
½ teaspoon salt
About 16 small whole
   canned jalapeños (not
   pickled), drained, cut
   into thick shreds
White Rice (page 74)

HEAT OIL in large heavy saucepan over medium-high heat. Brown pork in batches – do not overcrowd pan or pork will steam rather than brown – and remove to a plate.

Add garlic and onion, adding a little more oil if necessary and cook for 2 minutes or until tender. Reduce heat, add flour, and cook for 2 minutes, stirring constantly. Stir in chicken stock and bring to a boil, stirring. Return pork to pan, cover, reduce heat to medium-low, and simmer for 1 hour or until tender. Add salt and chiles and heat through. Serve the stew over rice in soup bowls. Serves 4.

Very simple, very delicious, very hot, and very comforting, this homey dish is comprised of nothing more than stewed pork chunks with onion, garlic, and shreds of chiles. ♦ White rice is the perfect accompaniment.

L ittle meats – carnitas – are the ultimate filling for tacos, burritos, or enchiladas. ◆ Pork is first braised to produce extremely tender meat, then baked to give nice crispy edges. Wrap the still warm meat in warmed flour tortillas, adding your favorite toppings – Tomato Salsa (page 25), Guacamole (page 27), chopped green onions, cilantro, chiles, sour cream, and cheese. ◆ Carnitas also make a simple dinner served with rice, salsa, and guacamole. ◆ For best flavor, serve carnitas fresh and warm; much flavor is lost once it's refrigerated.

CARNITAS

3 pounds boneless pork shoulder or butt	1 teaspoon salt
4 cups chicken stock	2 teaspoons ground cumin
1 medium onion, quartered	2 teaspoons dried oregano
4 large garlic cloves, peeled and left whole	¼ teaspoon cayenne

PLACE PORK in large saucepan; add chicken stock, onion, garlic, salt, cumin, and oregano and enough water to barely cover meat.

Bring to a boil, cover, reduce heat, and simmer for 2 hours or until meat is very tender.

Preheat oven to 400°F.

Transfer meat to baking dish, reserving broth for another use. Sprinkle with cayenne, and bake, uncovered, for 30 minutes or until meat is nicely browned. While still warm, shred meat with 2 forks, discarding fat. Serve warm. Serves 4 to 6.

MEXICAN MACARONI

2 cups elbow macaroni
¼ cup (2 ounces/½ stick)
  butter
1 tablespoon vegetable oil
1 large garlic clove,
  chopped
1 medium onion, chopped
½ pound (about
  12 medium) ripe cherry
  tomatoes, chopped
½ cup pickled sliced
  jalapeños, chopped

½ teaspoon dried oregano
½ teaspoon salt
Freshly ground black
  pepper
¾ pound extra-sharp
  Cheddar cheese, grated,
  plus several thin slices for
  topping
1 cup milk

PREHEAT OVEN to 450°F.

Cook macaroni in plenty of boiling water until tender but still al dente. Drain very well and transfer to 1½-quart baking dish. Stir in butter until combined; set aside.

Heat oil in small nonstick skillet over medium-high heat. Add garlic and onion and cook for 2 minutes or until tender. Add tomatoes, chiles, oregano, salt, and pepper and cook for 3 minutes or until tomatoes are softened. Stir mixture into noodles, then stir in grated cheese. Pour in milk; do not stir. Arrange slices of cheese on top. Bake, uncovered, for 30 minutes or until cheese is bubbly and lightly flecked with golden brown. Serves 4 to 6.

I *must confess that I really like macaroni and cheese and this, I think, is the ultimate. The addition of colorful tomatoes and chiles brings this simple, everyday dish to delectable heights.*

Salmon is wonderful grilled and served with this appealing pineapple sauce. ♦ The tangy salsa is also tasty with grilled poultry.

GRILLED SALMON WITH PINEAPPLE SALSA

1½ cups coarsely chopped peeled and cored pineapple (not canned)
1 large ripe papaya, peeled, seeded, and coarsely chopped
¼ cup chopped cilantro leaves
3 tablespoons chopped pickled jalapeños
1 tablespoon fresh lime juice

¼ teaspoon salt
¼ cup olive oil
2 tablespoons fresh lime juice
2 fresh salmon fillets (about 2 pounds)
Salt
Freshly ground black pepper

AT LEAST ONE HOUR in advance prepare salsa: put coarsely chopped pineapple and papaya in food processor and process for 2 to 3 seconds only just to coarsely purée – it shouldn't be totally smooth. Combine pineapple mixture, cilantro, chiles, lime juice, and salt in nonreactive bowl; chill.

Combine oil and lime juice in small bowl. Prepare charcoal fire and when coals are red-hot, sprinkle salmon with salt and pepper and brush both sides with oil mixture. Grill for 3 minutes each side, basting frequently, or just until opaque; do not overcook. Serve at once with salsa. Serves 4.

SEAFOOD CHILI

1 pound shrimp, peeled
  and deveined
½ pound bay scallops
1 tablespoon vegetable oil
4 large garlic cloves,
  chopped
1 medium onion, chopped
¼ cup sliced pickled
  jalapeños, chopped

28-ounce can Italian plum
  tomatoes, undrained
1 teaspoon best-quality
  chili powder
1 teaspoon salt
1 teaspoon dried oregano
1 cup loosely packed
  cilantro leaves, chopped
White Rice (page 74)

COOK SHRIMP and scallops in boiling water for 1 minute or just until opaque; drain and set aside.

Heat oil in large nonstick skillet over medium-high heat. Add garlic and onion and cook for 2 minutes or until tender. Add chiles, tomatoes, including liquid, chili powder, salt, and oregano; reduce heat to medium and simmer for 10 minutes or until sauce thickens slightly.

Add shrimp and scallops and cook for 2 minutes or just until heated through; do not overcook. Stir in cilantro and serve at once over rice in warmed wide shallow bowls. Serves 4 to 6.

A *lighter, rather more refined variation of beef chili (chili con carne), this succulent shrimp and scallop stew is deliciously pungent with cilantro.*

s l i c e d

p l a n t a i n s

SIDE DISHES

◆ ◆ ◆

Many Americans erroneously call this dish Spanish rice. ◆ A mainstay of the Mexican table, it's a wonderful, hot and spicy accompaniment which typically includes peas and diced carrots. Personally, I prefer it without these additions, but you may add them if you like.

MEXICAN RED RICE

1 tablespoon vegetable oil
1 small onion, finely chopped
2 large garlic cloves, chopped
1 cup long-grain rice (not parboiled or converted)
½ pound (about 12 medium) ripe cherry tomatoes, puréed in food processor

2 tablespoons chopped pickled jalapeños
1½ cups chicken stock
½ teaspoon salt
2 tablespoons chopped cilantro leaves

HEAT OIL in heavy medium saucepan over medium-high heat. Add onion and garlic and cook for 2 minutes or until tender. Stir in rice, then add puréed tomatoes, chiles, chicken stock, and salt. Bring to a boil, cover, and reduce heat to low. Cook for 25 minutes or until rice is tender and liquid is absorbed. Remove from heat and stir in cilantro. Serves 4.

BAKED RICE WITH CHEESE AND CHILES

2 tablespoons butter
2 large garlic cloves, finely chopped
1 small onion, finely chopped
1 cup Basmati or long-grain rice (not parboiled or converted)
2 cups water

1 teaspoon salt
½ cup sour cream
¼ cup chopped cilantro leaves
½ cup pickled sliced jalapeños, coarsely chopped
1 cup grated Monterey Jack cheese (4 ounces)

MELT BUTTER in heavy medium saucepan over medium-high heat. Add garlic and onion and cook for 2 minutes or until tender. Stir in rice, add water and salt, and bring to a boil. Reduce heat to low, cover, and cook, stirring occasionally, for 25 minutes or until liquid is absorbed and rice is tender. Transfer rice to greased 8-inch square glass baking dish and allow to cool thoroughly.

Preheat oven to 425°F.

Stir sour cream and cilantro into rice until combined, then chiles and grated cheese. Bake, uncovered, for 20 minutes or until heated through and lightly flecked with golden brown. Do not overcook. Serves 4.

Combining rice with a cheesy chile, cilantro, and sour cream mixture makes an indescribably tantalizing side dish. ◆ This is truly one of my favorite rice concoctions.

Mexican rice is rarely unseasoned, but I like to serve plain white rice with spicy or saucy dishes.

WHITE RICE

1 cup long-grain rice   ½ teaspoon salt
1½ cups water

PLACE RICE in strainer; wash thoroughly by rinsing under cold running water, swirling rice with your hands several times, until water runs clear.

Bring rice, 1½ cups water, and salt to a boil in medium saucepan over high heat. Reduce heat to medium-low, cover, and cook for 25 minutes or until rice is tender and liquid is absorbed. Remove from heat and allow to stand, covered, for 5 minutes before serving. Remove cover and fluff up with fork if desired. Serves 2 to 4.

P*ungent with cilantro and hot with chiles, this Mexican side dish definitely awakens the taste buds. ◆ Stir in a tablespoon or so of butter just before serving to tame the fire somewhat, if you wish.*

HOT GREEN RICE

3 large garlic cloves
¼ cup pickled sliced
  jalapeños
1 large green onion, cut in
  three

1 cup cilantro leaves
2 tablespoons vegetable oil
1 cup long-grain rice
1½ cups water
1 teaspoon salt

PURÉE GARLIC, chiles, green onion, and cilantro in food processor. Heat oil in heavy medium saucepan over medium-high heat. Add puréed mixture and cook for 1 minute. Stir in rice, then water and salt. Bring to a boil, cover, reduce heat to medium-low, and simmer for 30 minutes or until liquid is absorbed and rice is tender. Serves 4.

C

hiles pair so well with corn –
you can taste Mexico in each
delicious bite.

CORN WITH CHILES

2 tablespoons butter
1 garlic clove, chopped
¼ cup pickled sliced
   jalapeños, chopped

2 cups frozen corn kernels
   (12-ounce package)

MELT BUTTER in medium nonstick skillet over medium-high heat. Add garlic and cook for a few seconds. Add chiles and cook for 1 minute more. Stir in corn and cook, stirring, for 3 minutes or just until heated through. Serve at once. Serves 4.

emarkably refreshing, this dish is delicious prepared with either fresh or frozen corn kernels. ◆ It complements many dishes, grilled meats and poultry in particular. The salsa must be served promptly once it's prepared.

CORN, CHILE, AND TOMATO SALSA

1 cup fresh or frozen corn
   kernels, thawed
6 ripe cherry tomatoes,
   coarsely chopped
1 large whole green onion,
   chopped

2 tablespoons chopped
   pickled jalapeños
Salt

COMBINE ALL ingredients in serving bowl and serve at once. Serves 2 to 4.

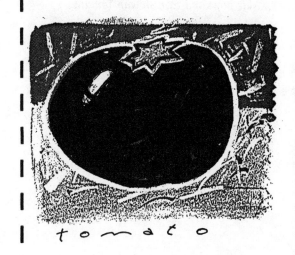

tomato

I n Mexico, beans are traditionally served as an accompaniment to everyday meals.
Pinto beans, and their
cousins, pink beans, are preferred in the
north, black beans in the south (they're
all delicious). ♦ These beans form the
basis of many dishes: refried beans
(frijoles refritos), stews, and soups. ♦ To
serve the beans as a homey soup, simply
put some beans with their liquid in a
wide bowl and garnish with Tomato
Salsa (page 25), chopped chiles, sour
cream, and cilantro. ♦ Lard is essential
for authentic flavor.

BASIC BEANS

2 cups (1 pound) dried black or pinto beans, rinsed and debris removed	1 large garlic clove, chopped
	1 small onion, chopped
	2 tablespoons lard
6 cups water	1½ teaspoons salt

PLACE BEANS in large bowl, add water to cover by about
2 inches, and soak overnight; drain beans, discarding soaking water.

Put beans in large heavy saucepan. Add 6 cups fresh cold
water, garlic, onion, and lard; bring to a boil. Reduce heat to
low, cover, and simmer for 1 hour or until very tender but
not mushy. Add salt only when beans are tender. (Adding
salt before then may toughen them.) Makes about 8 cups
(including liquid) or 5 cups beans.

Refried Beans

¼ cup lard
¼ cup pickled sliced
  jalapeños, chopped
  (optional)

Basic Beans (page 78)
1 to 1½ teaspoons salt

MELT LARD in medium nonstick skillet over medium-high heat. Add chiles and cook for 2 minutes or until tender. Add beans with about ½ cup bean liquid and a little pickled chile juice for extra zest, if desired, and mash with a potato masher until smooth but still chunky. Cook, stirring constantly, for 10 to 12 minutes or until mixture becomes a thick purée and crust forms on the bottom. Add salt to taste. Makes about 4 cups.

Refried beans are not really fried twice, just once. ◆ This rich and tasty bean paste is the ubiquitous accompaniment to Mexican and Southwestern dishes. Though canned ones are very good and I always have a can on hand, I still like to make them myself on occasion. Refried beans make an excellent filling for tacos, enchiladas, and burritos. As well, the beans are quite scrumptious adorned with a mixture of a little Cheddar and Monterey Jack cheese, then baked until the cheese is melted and bubbly; or top with crumbled feta or Parmesan cheese. ◆ Lard is essential for authentic flavor and besides, it has less cholesterol than butter – or so they tell me.

F

ried plantains make a
delicious side dish to Chicken
in Chile Chocolate Sauce
(page 58).

FRIED PLANTAINS

2 ripe but firm plantains   Salt
Vegetable oil for frying

TO PEEL PLANTAINS, use a sharp knife and slice off top and
tail. Make 3 or 4 lengthwise slits in skin without cutting
flesh. Peel back and remove skin. Slice plantains into
¼-inch rounds.

Heat thin film of oil in medium nonstick skillet over
medium heat. Add plantains and cook, turning occasionally, for 4 minutes or until tender and golden brown. Transfer to paper towel-lined plate to drain, sprinkle with a little
salt; serve at once. Serves 4.

Z *ucchini, corn, and sweet red peppers, when combined, transform into a delicious-tasting dish.*

ZUCCHINI, CORN, AND RED PEPPER SAUTÉ

1 tablespoon vegetable oil
2 large garlic cloves, chopped
1 small onion, chopped
1 small sweet red pepper, seeded and diced
1 medium zucchini, cut into ¼-inch slices

1 cup fresh or frozen corn kernels, thawed
¾ teaspoon dried oregano
Salt
Freshly ground black pepper

HEAT OIL in large nonstick skillet over medium-high heat. Add garlic, onion, and red pepper and cook for 2 minutes or until tender. Add zucchini and cook for 3 minutes or just until cooked through. Stir in corn, oregano, salt, and pepper and cook for 2 minutes or until heated through. Serves 4.

Limes

DESSERTS

♦ ♦ ♦

L uscious mango mousse takes minutes to make, a few hours to chill, and looks very pretty served in stemmed dessert glasses sprinkled with toasted coconut.

MANGO MOUSSE

2 large (2½ pounds) ripe
   mangos, peeled and fruit
   cut off pits

1 cup heavy cream
¼ cup shredded sweetened
   coconut

PURÉE MANGO in food processor – you should have about 2 cups.

Whip cream until it holds peaks, then fold into mango. Spoon into individual stemmed dessert glasses and chill.

Meanwhile, add coconut to small nonstick skillet and cook over medium-high heat, shaking pan and stirring constantly, until toasted; be careful not to overbrown. Set aside to cool.

Sprinkle each portion with toasted coconut just before serving. Serves 4.

MARGARITA PIE

1½ cups graham cracker
   crumbs
½ cup (4 ounces/1 stick)
   butter, melted
2 tablespoons sugar
4 eggs
1 cup sugar
¼ cup (2 ounces/½ stick)
   butter, melted

Grated zest of 1 lime
¼ cup fresh lime juice
¼ cup tequila
¼ cup Cointreau
Grated zest of 1 lime tossed
   with a little sugar
Whipped cream

PREHEAT OVEN to 350°F.

Thoroughly combine cracker crumbs, butter, and sugar in medium bowl; pat and press mixture on bottom and up side of 9-inch pie plate.

Whisk eggs, sugar, butter, lime zest, lime juice, tequila, and Cointreau in large bowl until blended. Pour mixture into crust and place pie on baking sheet to catch possible drips. Bake for 30 minutes or just until set; do not overcook. Allow to cool to room temperature, garnish with sugared lime zest, cover loosely with plastic wrap, and chill thoroughly before serving. Serve wedges of pie with whipped cream. Makes 1 9-inch pie.

A*n irresistible, luscious creation.*
♦ *It's best to prepare this pie a day ahead to allow the flavors to blend.*

I love shortbread cookies *(especially the cookie dough!).* ◆ *These Mexican shortbread cookies are delicious with pecans and orange zest.*

MEXICAN WEDDING COOKIES

1 cup butter (8 ounces/
   2 sticks) butter, at room
   temperature
½ cup confectioners' sugar
1 teaspoon vanilla
1 teaspoon finely grated
   orange zest
⅛ teaspoon salt
2 cups all-purpose flour
½ cup finely chopped
   pecans, toasted and
   cooled
Confectioners' sugar

PREHEAT OVEN to 325°F.

Cream butter and sugar in large bowl of electric mixer until soft. Beat in vanilla, orange zest, salt, and flour just until smooth and a piece of dough, when squeezed lightly, holds together. Stir in nuts.

Shape dough into 1-inch balls and place about 1 inch apart on ungreased cookie sheet. Flatten slightly with the bottom of a glass (if dough sticks too much, chill for 30 minutes or until easy to handle). Bake for 20 minutes or until edges are golden brown. Transfer to rack and, using a tiny sieve, generously dust cookies with confectioners' sugar. Makes about 2 dozen.

DRINKS

♦ ♦ ♦

This fabulous-looking, sublime-tasting piña colada is served in a toasted coconut-rimmed goblet instead of with the typical, tacky pineapple garnish. ♦ This makes 1 drink, though the amount of toasted coconut will do about 8. ♦ I recommend frozen – not canned – pineapple juice; it's fresher tasting.

pineapple

PIÑA COLADA

½ cup sweetened shredded coconut

3 ounces coconut cream plus extra for rimming glass

3 ounces pineapple juice

3 ounces light rum

Crushed ice (about 6 ice cubes)

TOAST SHREDDED COCONUT in medium nonstick skillet over medium-high heat, shaking pan and stirring constantly; be careful not to overbrown. Place on small dish.

Before stirring or shaking the coconut cream, spoon out a few tablespoons of the thicker liquid onto another small dish. Mosten ½ inch of outside rim of goblet in coconut cream, dip moistened rim in toasted coconut to coat, and set aside coconut side down for about 1 minute to allow it to set; chill glass if desired.

Put coconut cream, pineapple juice, rum, and crushed ice in blender and blend until frothy. Pour into prepared glass and serve at once. Makes 1 drink.

MARGARITA

Lime wedge
Salt
1½ ounces tequila
1½ ounces Triple Sec

1½ ounces fresh lime juice
Crushed ice (about 6
    cubes)

USE LIME WEDGE to moisten rim of 1 stemmed cocktail glass. Place salt on small dish; dip moistened rim into salt to coat; chill glass.

In blender, blend tequila, Triple Sec, and lime juice until frothy. Place crushed ice in salt-rimmed glass and pour mixture over ice. Serve at once. Makes 1 drink.

My version of this positively thirst-quenching cocktail is tart and not too sweet and partners perfectly with spicy foods. ♦ For a frozen margarita, blend the crushed ice along with the liquid mixture. This makes 1 drink; to make a pitcherful, use a few lime wedges to moisten 8 stemmed cocktail glasses, dip them into salt, and chill. Combine 1½ cups each, tequila, Triple Sec, lime juice, and crushed ice in a large pitcher, then blend mixture – in batches – until frothy, and pour into the prepared glasses.

An exquisitely refreshing drink for a warm summer evening or to serve with spicy foods. ◆ *Use a dry fruity Beaujolais or light red wine.*

SANGRIA

¾ cup fresh orange juice
⅓ cup sugar
1 bottle (750 ml) chilled
  red wine
2 cups chilled club soda
2 thin-skinned oranges,
  thinly sliced, then
  quartered

2 cups hulled, sliced ripe
  strawberries
Ice cubes

STIR ORANGE JUICE and sugar in large pitcher to dissolve sugar. Add wine, club soda, oranges, strawberries and ice cubes; stir well. Pour into ice-filled glasses and serve at once. Makes 1 large pitcher.

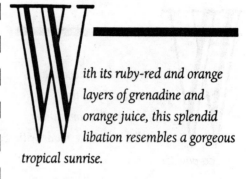

ith its ruby-red and orange layers of grenadine and orange juice, this splendid libation resembles a gorgeous tropical sunrise.

TEQUILA SUNRISE

¾ ounce grenadine
Crushed ice (about 6 ice
   cubes)

1 ounce tequila
4 ounces fresh orange juice

POUR GRENADINE over crushed ice in a stemmed cocktail glass. Pour tequila over grenadine, then add orange juice. Makes 1 drink.

W*ith its rich and chocolatey flavor, you'll find this sooo much smoother and darker than hot chocolate made with cocoa powder.*

MEXICAN HOT CHOCOLATE

4 ounces semisweet
  chocolate
3 tablespoons sugar
¼ teaspoon ground
  cinnamon

1 teaspoon vanilla
4 cups milk

COMBINE ALL INGREDIENTS in heavy medium saucepan. Bring just to a boil, stirring, over high heat. Carefully ladle about 1¼ cups mixture into a blender. Process until frothy and pour into cup or mug. Continue blending, one serving at a time. Serve at once. Serves 4 to 6.

angy, fresh limeade is a refreshing accompaniment to Mexican meals.

Limeade

½ cup liquid honey   4 cups very cold water
¾ cup fresh lime juice   20 ice cubes

POUR HONEY into large pitcher, add lime juice, and stir very well until honey is dissolved. Add cold water, and stir until combined. Add ice cubes, stir, and pour into tall ice-filled glasses. Serve at once. Makes about 4 servings.

INDEX

INDEX

◆ ◆ ◆